KINDLE PUBLISHING BUSINESS

A PATH TO BUILD A PUBLISHING BUSINESS AND A PASSIVE INCOME OF $10K A MONTH

Phil Johnson

Copyright © 2015 by D/O Publishing

Introduction

Congratulations! You've just made the first step in getting your life back! Like you, I worked 8 hours a day (plus an hour lunch), sat in traffic for 45 minutes to and from work, and made enough money to pay the bills. In the rarest of occasions, I'd make a little more than that. I spent so much of my time working so hard to get so little in return.

Sure, I liked my job. I worked with great people and had a great manager team. Sadly, nice people don't pay the bills. Our lives tend to run on cash-o-lene.

I spent hours every night when I got off work looking for a job that paid 2X more than my current job plus benefits, but unless I had a degree in brain surgery, there was little chance of making that. It was scary. The cost of college, the house, the car, and the normal day to day expenses had caught up with me. I worked so hard to build this suburban life that it was literally killing me!

One night I did some soul searching. I scoured the internet until I found something that I thought could help me. My wife had gone to bed hours before, and I was up until 3 AM, reading and searching. Then I found something on publishing books on Kindle. A man had started with close to nothing and built a "passive" income to make $20k a month.

Personally, that seemed too good to be true, but I kept reading. The more I read, the more feasible it became. It was something I knew I could do. I told my wife and a few friends about it, and I half expected them to think I was crazy. I am wise enough to have a good read on my friends, and they did think I was crazy

My Wife was very skeptical. It all seemed too good to be true. She told me she'd wait until I made money before she got excited. She was used to me making a small income online, but it wasn't a lot to brag about. I was a songwriter who wrote songs as gifts. I would get a job every couple weeks, and it brought in a couple hundred extra dollars. It wasn't enough. I needed more.

So I went all in. I put what little money I had (and didn't have) and dedicated all of my free time. No more video games; no more hanging out with friends. I was going to conquer this.

This book is going to:

- Break down the Kindle Publishing Process
- How to do your research
- Give tips on how to write your book or hire a writer to write your book
- How to pick a title that pops
- How to get a professional Ebook cover made

- How to promote your book effectively
- Tips to build your brand.

The first thing I want to address is that this is not a "get rich quick" scheme, and it is not a pyramid scheme. This book is showing you how to become a publishing business. I'm going to assume you're not made of money and not suggest the most expensive ways possible to do this business. Like you, I had very little disposable income. It took a lot of work early on but once the snowball got rolling, I was able to stop pumping my own money into it, and the business ran itself.

Let's go into what Kindle Publishing really is.

Chapter 1: Overview

The first time I tell someone about Kindle Publishing, they look at me in disbelief and treat me as if I'm selling phone cards. I think the only reason why they humor me is that I have a ton of passion for it. My eyes light up and I become a presenter. I have the ability to make anyone a believer when I'm talking face to face. But the truth is, it's not that far-fetched an idea. It's a business model that's been around for hundreds of years.

What you are essentially doing is creating a publishing company. You write or hire writers to make a book, you slap a nice cover on it and put it on sale. The difference between you and the thousands of publishers from the last one hundred years, is that you don't have to wait for your book to get pressed and printed, spending thousands of dollars up front and then wait months before finding out if your book was a hit or not.

It's as quick as clicking on a "publish" button and 12 hours later you have a book for sale. You could be making money within the first few hours! The whole point of this book is creating a kind of ritual that can help you regulate the process so that it doesn't feel random and you don't get overwhelmed.

Let's talk about how we do this thing in order, and then we'll break down each of those steps into more, detailed explanations. It's important to see if you like the general overview of the process before I drag you along on something that isn't quite up your alley and then you destroy the book because you're mad at me. That isn't the goal. The goal is to make money and to work smart, not hard.

The first part of the process is to get on amazon.com and search the Kindle best sellers. We will do research finding out what niches and topics are selling well. You can usually tell what the income potential is based on the book ranking. The closer you are to a #1 best seller, the more money you're going to make.

Once you find the niche that you're going to write about, you will either make an outline of the book and write the book yourself or hire a writer to write the book for you. The Ebooks don't have to be 300 pages long either. We're talking short informative books that are 7k words or more... But we'll go into that in more detail in the coming chapters.

Once your book is finished, you'll have to pick a title that's going to stand out and tell the reader why they want it. From there, you will either make a cover or hire someone to make a cover for you. The cover can make or break the sales of your book so it's important we get someone with experience to make it well!

After you receive the cover, we will format the book so that Kindle can present your book exactly the way you want it.

Then we'll create a KDP account with Amazon to submit your book. Once published, there are some free ways to promote your book with Amazon so that you can get hundreds or thousands of downloads.

Then we'll discuss ways to get reviews for your books because positive reviews are the lifeblood of sales on Amazon. If you have 1 or 2 stars, there is little chance anyone will buy your book.

Once your book is on sale and you're done with your promotions, you create more books!

I come from the songwriting world so I have experience with getting royalties. I would write an album, submit it to licensing companies, they'd get the song placed on a TV show and I'd be paid twice a year for it. I would never know what I was going to make until a few days before I received my check. The income was so sporadic. There were a lot of surprise moments when I would get a check for four or five thousand dollars.

What was neat about the process was once I had recorded a song and turned it in, I didn't have to do any more work. People just continued to use my songs and I made money from it. Kindle Publishing is exactly the same thing... except a lot less sporadic.

When you release a book, it's in the store forever! It's important to write good books because good books live the test of time. If you put out garbage, people will rate it lowly and your book will fall off the face of the earth.

When you put out good books about topics people want to read about, you will make money. It's definitely a business where you must have quality AND quantity. You never know what book is going to hit it big so it's important that you write a lot of good books on good niches.

Let's look at the numbers for a bit to put all of this into perspective.

If you have one book for sale that sells one a day at $2.99, you'll make 70% of that with Amazon. So for rounding purposes, we'll say you make $2 per book. If you sell one book a day for the average 30 days per month, you'll make $60. That's not that much money. That hardly seems worth it. Well, $60 dollars a month X 12 months out of the year equals $720 a year. Still not impressed?

Well, what if you had ten books a year making that much money? $7,200 a year. Still not satisfied? What if a hundred books a year made you that much?

$72,000 a YEAR. Do you make that now? That's $6,000 a month. I don't know about you, but I'm pretty sure my life would be a whole lot better if I had that kind of cheddar coming in!

Let's come back to the real world for a second. Not every book is going to sell one a day. I know this. Your competition knows this. You'll find that you're going to make 80% of your money from 20% of your books.

In my very first month of Kindle Publishing, I put out 12 books. I wrote 7 of them and paid writers for the other 8. 5 of them sold more than 2 a day each. The others sold one every other day or every other 2 days.

In my first month, I had spent $500 to jumpstart my business. That was to pay for writers, get covers made, hire a virtual assistant, and pay for website memberships to make my job easier. Again, you don't HAVE to spend that kind of money to get this started. I wanted to see if I could make it happen, so I ramped up quick to get to 12 books.

In my first month, I made $250. So I lost money. I remember telling a few co-workers about my first month and they laughed. It was as if they knew I was going to fail. Except... I didn't fail. The following month, I decided to hold back paying for writers and challenged myself to write 2 books a week about really good niches. My books from the month earlier made me another $250 PLUS I made an additional $400 from my new books because I got better at picking niches. Then the following month, I did that same thing and was making $1500 a month. Then I took the $1500 and put all of it back into the business hiring writers, a Virtual Assistant, and an in-house cover maker and I made $3,000 the following month. I barely did anything!

The point is in the beginning it takes time and excitement to build this business. Once you get it going, it will snowball and you'll go from spending 20-30 hours a week on it to 4 hours a week.

Once you get it going at full capacity, you feel strangely powerful. You have your own publishing company with employees and you're instantly a business person. How crazy is that?

It was a bittersweet moment when I walked into my job of 4 years and told them it was time for me to leave. I was making double my income with Kindle Publishing. A lot of my doubters watched in disbelief. Soon after, all my old co-workers wanted to get in on it.

I didn't get rich quick. It took discipline to not spend my early profits on myself. I had to show self-control and put all the money I received back into the business. I did that for 3 months in a row. Then once I made $3,000 a month, I kept $1,000 for myself and left $2,000 to cover my expenses every month. My expenses never grew much more than that, but my profit did.

I wasn't in a pyramid scheme. I didn't have to pay anybody anything if I didn't want to. I invested my own time and money. I paid writers to write books for me that I kept the rights to and it kept them busy and gave them jobs. Sometimes their books made me money, sometimes they didn't. I took all the risk.

What I hope you get out of this overview is that it is a time commitment. I recommend you get your hands dirty early so that you can learn the entire process. Once you learn to be successful with it yourself, that's when you hire others to take your place. It's hard to know if someone is doing a good job if you, yourself doesn't know what that looks like.

All I can say is that if you stay the course, you can and will make money. Write good content and you'll make money on it for years to come. If you make bad content, you won't be around long.

Look at this opportunity as a way to help people. Money is secondary.

Chapter 2: Keyword Search

Before you write your bestseller book, it's important to see what is selling well in the Kindle Store. Sure, you could take the "shotgun" approach and spend a bunch of time writing books in a bunch of miscellaneous topics hoping that someone will be interested in buying your books, but why take that chance and waste time and money? If you're doing this, you have to think like a business person.

What I love about Amazon is that most of your tools you need to be successful will be on the site itself. You don't have to pay someone to go do research for you. All you need is an internet connection, access to amazon.com and patience!

Go to amazon.com and look at the search bar. Click the ALL button and a drop-down menu will appear. Scroll down and click on Kindle Store. Then hit the Search Button to the right.

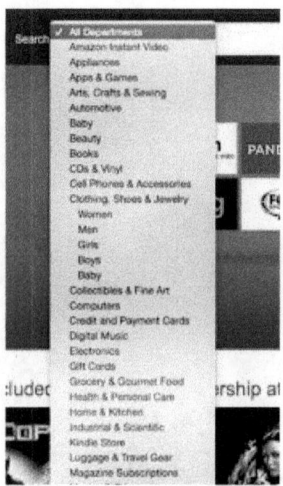

Once you hit the search button, click on the Kindle eBooks link at the top of the page next to the Buy A Kindle tab.

After you clicked Kindle Ebooks, you'll see a bunch of books on the screen. Click on the Best Sellers link showed here:

You will then be looking at a page that shows the best sellers in Kindle Ebooks. You'll see a Top 100 Paid and Top 100 Free. This is the first place to want to look to do your Niche Research.

You have the option to make both fiction and nonfiction books. While fiction books sell the best on Kindle, the easiest ones to make money from are non-fiction books.

Fiction

Fiction books are stories that aren't real. They can be about anything from the Zombie Apocalypse to erotica. The hard part about writing fiction is that you have to be good at writing it. You NEED a creative mind!

Growing up, I always wanted to write a book about horror stuff like R.L Stein did with his Goosebumps books. It always seemed so far out of reach. When I started doing Kindle Publishing, the 4th book I put out was a fiction story about the zombie apocalypse. I wrote it in a day and it ended up outselling my first three books 5 to 1.

If you're a creative type, I say go for it!

Non-Fiction

In the last chapter, I mentioned that you want to solve your reader's problem. The best way to do this is with non-fiction or "real information" books. Think of a problem somebody may have... How can you solve that problem? The great thing about non-fiction is that the answer is probably somewhere on the internet, and with some rewriting skills, you can gather the information within an hour or two and write the book rather quickly.

So for my example, I will search for something simple like "Positive Thinking." If you're following along with me near a computer, as I begin to type in "Positive" a bunch of suggestive words pop up. This can be one of your most useful tools. You're essentially given access to what most people are searching for. "Positive Thinking" is at the top but there is a bunch of extras that are there for me to explore at a different time.

I'll continue through with positive thinking. A bunch of books pop up, most have a handful of reviews. The top book that currently pops up on my screen has 684 4.5 star reviews as of the writing of this book.

When I click on the book, it takes me to a description page, showing the cover, the multiple ways I can buy it, the length and the best sellers rank.

The Best Sellers Rank

I'm going to tell you right now, this may be the single most important stat you need to look at when looking at a book. When you look at any book on Amazon, when you scroll down the page, you'll come to an area that starts with "Product Details." At the bottom of that list, you will see the "Amazon Best Sellers Rank" with a number beside it, as well as a couple numbers below that with sub-categories.

Amazon Best Sellers Rank: #14,327 Paid in Kindle Store (See Top 100 Paid in Kindle Store)
#35 in Kindle Store > Kindle eBooks > Nonfiction > Self-Help > **Happiness**
#62 in Kindle Store > Kindle eBooks > Nonfiction > Self-Help > **Motivational**

In the beginning, you want to keep a close eye on the sales number, especially if you don't have a lot of money to put into the business upfront. We want to minimize your risk as best as possible.

Essentially, if you find a niche where books are selling in the top 50,000, that's a niche that you want to enter. Don't waste your time on any niche above 100,000. In my experience, if you're between 50,000 and 100,000 you're selling anywhere from 2-4 books a day. That number only grows as you get closer to 1.

The first book I looked at is currently at #14,327. That's pretty good! They are selling anywhere from 15-20 a day.

So now I'm going to go back a page on Amazon and check out the next 2 books on the list and see where they stand.

The second book was at #32,527 and the third book was at #43,662. So clearly, this is a really good niche to get into. There isn't a lot of competition and frankly all the book covers look lame. This is a good opportunity for me to jump in there and get a piece of that pie!

Task

What I would recommend you do before you write a book on the very first niche you find, is find 10-15 niches that are averaging in the top #100,000 best sellers. The more niches to pick from the better you can feel about approaching the topic!

Chapter 3: Write a Book

Now that you've collected a handful of niches. Hopefully, you narrowed it down to one that you like. The cheapest way to write a book is to write it yourself. I suggest picking a topic that you know really well. The better you know something, the less you have to research and the fewer obstacles you'll have to face in putting it together.

For this book, I'm going to use the "Positive Thinking" topic since the sales have been stellar for the other books in the niche. I'm generally an optimistic guy so I have some good tips to keep the mind free. Plus a quick google search of "Positive Thinking" will give me a plethora of information to add to my book.

Research

If you're picking a niche you don't know all the ins and out of, it's important you research your topic before you write about it. Twenty years ago, this would have been a pain in the butt, but now with the power of the internet, all you have to do is read a few articles, collect the information and write it in your own words.

It's important to note that you should never copy and paste things from the internet and put it in your book as your words. That can lead down a dangerous road which could lead to you getting sued. Plus, it's morally wrong. That's no different than me breaking into your house and stealing your TV. Seriously DON'T STEAL! If you find information online that you believe is good info, write it in your own words.

If I know the topic I'm researching really well, sometimes all I'll do is write down the subtopic titles of the information I find online and then write my own version of it. That way I won't have to worry about accidentally copying.

Outline

Once you've gathered all your information before you sit to write your book, it's important you know the path you're going to take. It can be as light or as detailed as you want. The important part is that you know where you want to go. It also helps you keep track so you don't forget anything.

Most books will start with an introduction, then you'll face the meat of the content and then end with a conclusion. If you went to high school, you should know how to write papers using an outline method.

Personally, I just pull out notes on my iPhone and write down main topics like so:

Kindle Publishing

Overview

Keyword and Market Research

Write a Book

Hire Writer
- *where*
- *how to search*
- *how to interview*
- *how to scan*

Pick a great title

Order a Cover

How to Format Your Book

how to Submit to Kindle And promote

Getting reviews for your book
Creating an Author Central Page
Building a brand and make more money
Create more Books and scale

Think of it like you're writing a table of contents. There will be a lot of subtopics in each main topic but just be sure to make note of them.

Before You Write the Book

Now before you write the book, I think it's important that you don't psyche yourself out. It's intimidating when you tell yourself "I need to write a book today." That's a huge undertaking... Especially if you've never written a book before.

When I say book, the first thing that pops into your head is probably a novel sized book that is 200-300 pages long. While you're free to write those kinds of books, I'm going to tell you not to do that.

Your book only needs to be 25-30 pages longs. Sometimes more... maybe a little less. You're not writing textbooks here. In the Kindle age, people want to be able to read and get information quickly. They don't want to read a book full of fluff with information being rehashed 70 times over.

The word count on the type of book we're going to write will be no less than 6k word and no more than 12k. There are courses out there that will tell you that you can write books at 3,500 words, but I'm going to suggest strongly that you don't do that. Kindle has evolved over the last couple of years, and that small amount of words is just too little.

It's important not to get caught up in how many words you have in your book. Instead of asking "how many words do I absolutely need to write this book?" the question should be "Did I fix the reader's problem?"

My first book was 14,000 words. I wrote on a music topic that I had a lot of passion for. I just couldn't stop writing. Well, that book is sitting at slightly over 1,000,000. I sell 1 to 2 books a week.

On the flip side, I released a diet book at 6,000 words and it sells 3-4 a day. It has excellent reviews and people were satisfied paying $2.99 for it. Not all topics you write about will fit in 6,000 words. Hell, not all will fit in 12,000 words. If it doesn't, you can write another book on that topic! There's your more potential income!

The point is to not overwhelm yourself with the length. If you write an 8,000-word book, read it and say "yeah, this is straight to the point and answers the question" then you've done a good job.

It's also important to note that not all of your books will sell. Sometimes it has nothing to do with your writing ability. It's just the luck of the draw. Don't take it personally. That's why it's a quality AND quantity game. The more books you put out, the better chance you have of making more money.

Ways to write a book

Now that we got everything else out of the way let's look at ways to actually hammer this thing out!

Type it

I'm writing this book in Apple's Pages program. I'm a very fast typer. It's taken me 2 1/2 hours to write to this point. I tend to ignore the mistakes I make as I type so that I don't lose my train of thought. You'll always be able to go back and fix the mistakes later.

I sit on my computer and just type. My Wife thinks it's crazy that I can have a conversation with her, looking her in the eye while I type my thoughts onto the computer. It took me a lot of practice. Some people just can't type that fast. That's OK.

There are some programs out there like "Dragon speak" for Mac or PC where you can talk and the software will type it out for you. You have to speak your punctuation, however. For example:

How are you today question mark I'm doing very well exclamation point

    Which translates into:
How are you doing today? I'm doing very well!

It takes a little practice but it can save you a lot of time if you're not much of a typer. If you have a smartphone, you can easily do this.

With my iPhone or iPad, I use Pages and the built-in dictation feature when I don't feel like using my fingers to tap on a digital keyboard. Then I can pull the file up on my computer later and pick up where I left off.

Voice Record

One really cool technique that I've yet to do is record yourself. After you've written your outline, get a tape recorder, voice memo recorder or anything that can record you talking, hit record and just start talking. If you talk pretty steady for 3 or 4 hours, you'll more than hit your word target. Then you hit play and type out what you say.

If I weren't such a fast typer, this would probably be the way I would write books. I'm very conversational when I type and I imagine if I didn't have a keyboard in front of me right now, I'd talk this book out the same way.

If you have extra cash on hand and don't want to type out what you "spoke", you can hire someone to write it out for you and format it into a book.

Outsourcing

If you have a little extra money on the side and either don't feel up to writing a book or have no ability to do so, you can hire a writer to create a book for you. Honestly, you're eventually going to get to this step because while writing your own books can be fun and all, to truly ramp this business into something that becomes a "passive" income, you have to be able to remove yourself from necessary positions.

You can find writers in a handful of different places, but I'll focus on a couple specific websites to get you started.

Elance or Odesk

While the websites both look very different, they are now one company. Here you can post a job and search for writers by having them apply. The great thing about using a service like this is you're protected. You pay an "escrow" service that holds your money in limbo until you receive the work you paid for. Nobody gets screwed in this scenario. If the writer delivers garbage, you don't have to pay them.

When posting a job, it's important you spell out exactly what you want and expect. That way there are no surprises. For example:

Hey folks,

I'm a publishing company who focuses on non-fiction books that help people.
I'm currently looking for a native English speaking ghostwriter who can do an 8k word project for me.
This job could potentially turn into a long term relationship. I'm looking to build a small team of writers that I can give regular work too.

Please send me a sample of your best work.

Preference will go to anyone who charges $80 or less.

I check all work for plagiarism so please ORIGINAL WORK ONLY!

Who is the first president of the United States?

Thanks!

There are a couple parts I want to focus on so that you can see why I wrote what I wrote.

First and foremost, I asked for a native English speaking ghostwriter. Most of the writers on odesk and elance will be from countries where their English isn't on par with what we're used to. It's obvious from the very first paragraph you read. Normal readers can tell immediately. Make sure you get someone who understands our sentence structure.

I mentioned I'm looking for a long term relationship. This is key because the people who apply will want to impress someone who can essentially give them a full-time job.

I mentioned I would give preference to anyone who charged $80 or less. Honestly, I don't like to pay more than a dollar for every 100 words. You will get a lot of writers who will try to charge you $200-$400 and honestly, you don't need to spend that.

At the end of my job posting, I ask a random question to see if the person applying is reading my job posting and not just randomly applying.

You will get a handful of people who will apply with a large scale of prices. Sadly, even the sample work they send you could potentially be written by somebody else. I find that if you Skype interview them, you can get a good feel if they're a native English speaker or not.

Honestly, early on, you're going to have to go through bad eggs to get a good team together. If a writer sends you garbage, don't pay them for it. You're protected. If you find a writer who is awesome, don't let them go. I had gone through 2 bad writers before I got a team of 3 that I trust and can rely on,

epicwrite.com

Epicwrite is a website that has a staff of hired writers that you can pay to make the book for you. The difference of going this route instead of the other two is that you have no communication with the writer. You're not building a team. So even if you find someone brilliant, they're not yours to work with. I have heard in recent months that their quality has come down a bit, so use them at your own risk.

Editing Your Book

Whatever you do, do not release your book without some kind of editing. It doesn't need to be perfect, but the closer it is to perfect, the better reviews it will get and the better off you will be. It's important that you also check the book for plagiarism. Whether you wrote the book or someone else did, check it just in case.

grammarly.com

If you're writing the book yourself and are trying to save money where you can, I highly recommend you use this site. It's $30 a month (and you can get huge discounts if you sign up for longer), but it can save you so much time and fix so many overlooked problems. It isn't the perfect solution, but it makes suggestions on what words you can use that will be better in your sentences, it will check for plagiarism, and it will correct most grammar problems.

I do recommend you read your book as you use the program because some suggestions the website makes doesn't quite make sense.

Even if you hire writers, I think grammarly is a quick way to see if the writers plagiarized and it's an even quicker way to see if they know how to write at all. The website will tell you how much of the paper needs correcting based on a % rate. My first two bad writers came back with huge problems and I could tell without even reading it.

With the writers I trust now, it takes less than 5 minutes to fix any small problems they may have. Once you get a budget for a team, you can train a VA to do this for you.

Hire an Editor

If you have money on hand or live with someone who likes editing, having a fresh pair of eyes can help in ways a machine can't. First, they can tell you if they like it or not and second they can tell you if it sounds natural. If you have a disposable amount of money, paying someone $50 bucks isn't a half bad price to get an honest opinion.

Chapter 4: GET A COVER!

Growing up, most of us have been told "never judge a book by its cover." In Kindle, your cover can single-handedly bring your book sales to its knees. A good looking cover is NECESSARY! It has to catch an Amazon shopper's eye from a small thumbnail photo. If it doesn't, it will get lost in a sea of undesirable covers. Let's go through some essentials for a good cover!

A Good Title

The title has a pretty big bearing on if your book is something anyone would bother looking at. The title tells us in just a few words if this is indeed the book that is going to solve all our problems. In this business, one word isn't enough!

It's important that you have both a title and a sub-title. The title will highlight the main topic, and the subtitle will give more information.

To continue on the Positive Thinking train, let's call the book "Positive Thinking." It's ok if there are other books with the same title. The subtitle is where we can get creative. Personally I like to re-mention the title in some capacity in the subtitle if I can help it.

Amazon's search engine is one of the most powerful on the Internet, and keywords have a lot to do with if your book is successful. So If I mention Positive thinking twice in a title, isn't my book more likely to be discovered?

So for my subtitle I decided "A Guide to Think Positive and Attract Happiness from the Universe."

It explains what the book is about and I think it adds a little mystery because it has something to do with the universe in a tangible way.

Get the Cover Made

Unless you're a graphic designer or have a keen eye for book covers, I think it's best to trust your covers to the professionals. If you're not one to make covers, it will take you a long time to get it right and between you and me... your time is more valuable. So I hire someone to do my covers... and it's not expensive.

fiverr.com

This website is amazing. You can pick from hundreds of different types of jobs for as little as $5. That's Crazy talk you say? It's true. What if I told you I get 90% of my covers from this website?

All you do is search the extensive library of artists and pick someone who can make the perfect cover for you. For non-fiction books, covers don't have to be super complicated.

I always look for an artist who offers a free royalty free image to use for your cover. I do this because it can cost me more than $5 to buy an image. There is a handful of cover makers on Fiverr that spend some of their earnings on royalty-free web site memberships so that they're more likely to get your business. This is also ingenious because they give you the website link and they tell you to pick an image.

90% of the cover work is having the right image, and they're sending you to do that work to find what you want. Then when you find it, they pick the right font and text and send it to you within a few days. In most cases, they'll do unlimited revisions until you're happy.

elance.com or odesk.com

While Fiverr is a great way to get a cover, ultimately to stand out above the rest, you may want to invest in a cover maker for your team. I have one person I always go to when it comes time to making a fiction book cover. It costs me about $20 but when I need something a little extra special, it's worth it.

When I got into this business, everyone told me fiction was a hard market to get into. I wrote a 10k word book and had an awesome cover made for $20. In its first week, I made my money back without any promotion. That book continues to be one of my best sellers and I give 100% credit to that cover.

Below is a few example covers from my Publishing Company, D/O Publishing:

The covers really pop! I found really cool pictures and the fiverr.com artist did the rest. When it came to my competition, I stood out because I knew how to pick a cool title, and I had a good eye for eye-catching photos. It takes practice, but if there is any step you shouldn't skip over, it's the making a cover step. If you're not sure what photo to use, ask friends what sticks out to them.

Make sure the cover gets made to the dimensions of a Kindle book. Most fiverr.com artists know the dimensions. You just have to let them know in advance.

Chapter 5: Formatting a Book

This part of the book will be a little vague because there are so many programs that you could be writing your book on and honestly, I think there are better visual ways to learn the process.

youtube.com

There are literally dozens of videos that will show you how to format your document into a language that Kindle speaks. Anything from Word, Pages, Google Docs, and a handful of others.
Just search and you will find exactly what you need!

fiverr.com

I'm telling you, for five bucks, you can get almost anything done on this site. You can pay someone to format your book into a Kindle. Problem solved!

Internet

If you rather read it and follow along, my suggestion would be to google search and find one of the thousands of documents on the Internet that focus on formatting,

Suggestions

What I can say is that you don't want to write in straight paragraph form unless of course you are writing fiction. With non-fiction, you want to break topics and subtopics up. Putting bullet points can give the reader's eyes a break and make things a little more understandable. Explore the space on the paper and think back to some of your favorite non-fiction books. If you have the book near you, pick it up and investigate, and don't be afraid to borrow. There are only so many ways to format a book!

Chapter 6: Kindle Digital Publishing Explained

Now that your book is finished, it's time to get it in the hands of everyone who will take it so you can make lots and lots of money... as well as help people!

You sign up at KDP.Amazon.com with your Amazon account and use your Social Security Number (or whatever numbers they require if you live out of the United States). Signing up is self-explanatory.

Once your account is up and running, you'll be brought to the screen seen below. Let's go over what you'll use the most!

Bookshelf

This is the area where you will see all the books you have published or are in a queue to publish.

Reports

Here you will find what books have sold or have been borrowed. Detailed sheets will be shown as your books begin to be downloaded. From there, you can download excel sheets that show you what has been downloaded and how much you have made.

Add New Title

This is the button you push to start your journey into Kindle Publishing. Once you publish one, it's hard to stop! I imagine you'll hit that button a lot in the coming years!

Once you hit the "add new title" button you will be taken to a screen where you will enter your book information.

At the top of the screen, you will see a blue box that's telling you about KDP Select. We'll talk about that more in the next chapter. Continue passed that and go down to where you see "Getting started."

You'll be asked to enter the Book Name and Subtitle.

If your book is a part of a series, you can select so

Next, you will put the edition of the book. If it's your first, it's 1. As you make edits or add to the book as the years go on, you can change that number.

You will be asked to put in a Publisher name. I would suggest you pick a name you like and use it in all of your books. It helps make you and your books look legit, plus it can help you as you try to brand your books.

You will then be asked to write a description of your book. It's important that you make this as exciting as possible, and use HTML to add bold letters. Your description is second only to your cover. A boring description can be the reason somebody doesn't buy your book.

You will be asked to add a "contributor." That will be the Author name. You can either use your name or a pen name. It's really up to you. I used pen names for certain niches. My name has an authority in one niche, but I'm not sure someone would trust me in another niche. Sometimes I'll use female pen names and discover a book sells better because of it.

You will be asked to verify your publishing rights. Only ever do the "not a public domain work." Don't bother messing around with public domain work. It's not worth it, and there is so much red tape on the subject that you can get your account shut down if you make even one mistake.

Pick categories that you believe your book will best fit in. What's really neat about Amazon is if your book fits better in a 3rd or 4th category, Amazon will automatically put your book there.

You can pick an age range if you'd like. I only ever do this if I'm writing fiction books (most people use it when publishing erotica).

Pick up to 7 keywords or phrases. This can have a large impact on how your book pops up in the search bar. Be sure to pick keywords that you can rise in. For example, with Positive Thinking, I put

1. Positive Thinking
2. The Secret
3. The Universe
4. Human Sprit
5. Attract Happiness
6. How to think Positive
7. How to stop thinking negative

You are then asked if you'd like to put your book on Preorder or release it now. What you pick will depend on your marketing strategy.

You then will upload your cover (or launch a cover creator but DON'T DO THAT! It will look like garbage). Then you will upload your book. Once your book is uploaded, you can preview it on a Kindle book previewer. This is your chance to see how your book looks on a handful of Kindle reading devices. This is your LAST CHANCE to catch mistakes. Don't let your first negative review be that they can't read your book because it's formatted badly.

If the book looks good, you'll go onto pricing.

You'll verify what territories you want to sell in, but if you're in the business of making money, you'll just select Worldwide rights... All Territories. If you go down a little bit, you'll see a KDP Pricing Support. This will show price other books like yours have sold for and will make a suggestion so that you can make the most money.

Royalty Rate

Amazon has 2 royalty rates. 35% and 70%. How much do you want to make?

The way it's been set up is if you sell a book between $2.99 and $9.99, Amazon will pay you 70%. Why? Because with their expertise in the business they found that if you sell within this range, you'll sell the most, and it motivates sellers to keep their books affordably priced. Plus, Kindle books cost virtually 0 dollars to produce. You're not printing on paper!

If you price your book anywhere from $.99 to $2.98 or $10.00 and up, you will only get 35%. Sometimes it makes sense to sell your book at $.99. A dollar is nothing now a days and most people are willing to let it go easily.

What to Set Your Price At?

Obviously this is really up to you, but to stay competitive, I find if you're selling books between 7,000 words and 15,000 words, price the book at $2.99. That's less than a cup of coffee at Starbucks and most people won't return it even if they don't like it. You'll get $2 on every sale.

If you write a fiction series that ties into each other, it's sometimes worth selling the first book in the series for $.99 and then make lost money on purchases made on the future books. Think of that first book like a sales funnel.

Kindle Matchbook

As a first time author, you won't have much of these lying around but you can make it possible for customers with a physical copy of your book to get the Kindle version of your book for free or a $.99 cost. Don't be greedy. You should always look to help your customer where it isn't a problem for you. If they already supported you, give them a break!

Kindle Book Lending

This is something that's new to Kindle in the last couple of years. It lets your customer borrow your book. If they read more than 10% of your book, you get paid a royalty. The number paid fluctuates from month to month, but as of the time of this writing, the royalty rate was $1.40 per borrow.

I'll tell you why this is an amazing thing. No matter how high or low you price your book, you get this royalty rate. In my very first month of Kindle sales, I made more money in borrows than I did actual sales. Almost 2 to 1. That number only went higher! Look at this is a good thing and as an income you might not have gotten.

Publish Your Book

Hit that button and off it goes. It takes 12-48 hours but in my experience, it usually takes less than 8 hours. Then your published writer (or a publishing company if you hired your writer). This is a big step. The first one is the hardest and yet the most exciting. Nothing will quite be as meaningful as your first published book. Even if it doesn't make its money back, it will have been the one that was the most special.

Chapter 7: Kindle Promotions, Getting Reviews, and Branding
One of the best parts of Amazon's platform is that it has built-in promotion.

KDP SELECT

If you want the best free promotion possible, I highly recommend that you sign up for KDP Select. It's essentially a program that you enroll your book in for 60 days that promises that you won't sell it anywhere else but Kindle or Amazon. Honestly, with as much market share that Amazon has, you'd best just do it.

By enrolling, you're given two types of free promotions that you can use in every 60-day stint that you're enrolled in KDP Select. The Free Book Promotion and the Kindle Countdown Deal.

Free Promotion

This promotion gives you 5 days to make your book free and Amazon agrees to promote it on the free section of the site. This is an excellent way to get your book into as many hands as possible and it also gives you a window of opportunities to get reviews (more on this later).

Kindle Countdown Deal

Once your book has been out awhile, Kindle allows you to drop the price of your book for up to five days starting at $.99 and moving up in price day by day to the price you set, allowing you to keep 70% of the profit. This is huge because in normal circumstances you would only get to keep 35% of the royalties on $.99

Getting Reviews

There are many ways to get reviews for your book and I'll break down each of them here.

Organically

Organic reviews will probably be the most honest, but you'll end up waiting forever to get them. For every thousand times your book is downloaded, only one person will leave a review. Unless you write the hit of the century or the stinker of the decade. I can't imagine you'd get a lot of reviews early on. With no reviews, no one will want your book.

Paid Reviews

Exercise caution when going this route. It is against Amazon's Terms and Conditions to do this. If Amazon catches you in the act, they can and WILL shut down your account. That being said, You can pay people on fiverr.com to give you reviews for 5 bucks a piece. Just keep in mind, Amazon has spies waiting to catch you in the act!

Review Swaps

While this is against Amazon's TOC (If you exchange anything for a review, whether it's monetary or not, you can still get in trouble) this is probably the most popular. You find other authors or Virtual Assistants that are willing to do a review of your book if you are willing to do one for theirs. There's usually a mutual understanding that you will give either 4 or 5 stars. If you can't, let them know and don't swap.

In my experience, there is a ton of Facebook groups you can join where there are essentially hundreds of people swapping book reviews. Within my first two weeks, I built up an excel document with 60 people I could swap with at any given time. It was easy to get 15-20 reviews... But very time-consuming. After writing books, and promoting them, I got burned out fast. The first thing I outsourced to a Virtual Assistant was review swaps. It's easy work... but tedious.

Ask for Honest Reviews

Believe it or not, you can search for Amazon's top 1000 reviewers and ask them to read your book and give an honest review. Technically you're supposed to have them disclose that they were asked, but it shouldn't be a problem as long as you didn't pay them

My Strategy for Reviews

My strategy is simple. I put my book on Free promotion for 3 of my 5 available days. For those days, I promote and find as many people to swap with as possible, With my book being free, it's easy to swap. It's always harder when a book costs money.

I wait three days from the time I download an author's book until the time I write a review. Why? To avoid suspicion with Amazon!

If I download a book, open it and write a review 5 seconds after I download it, Amazon will pick up on that quick and delete my review.

I keep an excel sheet to stay organized, making sure I'm keeping track of whose book I downloaded, when I downloaded it, when I need to write the review, and a check mark to note if they indeed left a review on my book.

There's no exact right way to keep track. Each person is different. To avoid getting screwed, find an organized way to do this fast!

Do NOT review other people's books with the same Amazon Account as your Kindle Publishing account. Create a pseudo account and buy something for $.99 so that you can Leave verified reviews. Verified Reviews always hold more weight than non-verified reviews.

Branding

Author Central Page

Whether you write your own books under your own name or you write under a pen name, it's very important that you create an Author Central Page. This page allows you to post a picture of the author and give a quick blurb of who they are, This page also allows you to group every book written under that pen name.

Amazon will make suggestions like "Here are other books by this author..." and it promotes the author's other works. Imagine if you had a book about running a marathon by a pen name that also has a book about long distance swimming. What if the customer liked your book and was preparing for a triathlon. Boom, a second sale just like that! Never underestimate the power of branding.

Group Your Niches

It's very important that you don't go into Kindle Publishing shotgun shooting topics. Pick a niche and dominate. What does that mean? Say you want to write a book on Paleo and you put out a book on the Paleo Diet for Vegans. Write a paleo book for vegetarians, for Christmas, for summer, for athletes, etc. Dominate that niche and become an authority!

Another Strategy for Reviews

Some folks will price their book at $0.99 and do a swap with others who are also looking for 99 cent swaps. You may pay between $6-$10 to get your 6-10 reviews, and then put your book on free promo. Because the book has so many good reviews, people will download it much more often because it's free. The will move you up the ranks and when you put your book back on sale for $2.99, you'll be high in the sales ranker and make even more money.

Chapter 8: Scale

So you've released your first book. Maybe you released a small handful of books. Maybe you wrote them all yourself and it took a lot of time. You should be proud of what you've accomplished. A lot of people give up before they even begin.

For this business to truly become passive, you have to remove yourself from it. It can take up to 6 months for this to happen if you're releasing between 10-15 books a month,

It takes 60 days for Kindle to pay you from the end of your first month of sales. That means if you publish your first book on the 1st of the month, you won't be paid until 90 days after. That's a lot of time you have to put in with some money you'll have to contribute out of pocket.

The money you make will be theoretical because all it is is numbers and dots on a chart. It won't be real until you get the money. What will separate you from the people who fail is what you do with that first check. Take the check and put it back into the business.

On my first check, I got paid $250. I reinvested that into the business. That paid for all my covers and paid for my VA to do review swaps for me for the month.

The second check I made $650. That allowed me to cover the expenses of the first month, as well as get writers to write 6 books. So my writing time was cut in half.

My third check I made $1500 and I was able to have all my books written, pay my VA, and remove myself from writing (even thought I would write a book here or there because I liked it).

The 4th check I made $3000. This was the first month I was able to take some money as payment to pay myself, have all my business expenses covered and then some. It only got bigger and bigger.

Over time, I was able to hire a virtual assistant who became a project manager. They would manage my writers and VAs and essentially run my business. It was amazing. It was a well-oiled machine and I got richer by the day. I taught my VA how to do niche research and I had weekly meetings with my project manager. He would show me the numbers, what he had in the works for me, the costs, the reviews, and every other miscellaneous part of the organization.

It all makes sense because I started the business from the ground up, learning every little piece of it and teaching it out. I was then no longer CEO of my own company. I was an investor. I kept the cash flow going but put the business in capable hands.

Promote

There are different ways to promote your book! If youRe an avid user of Facebook, you can find groups that are related to your niche and promote there. There are tons of Free Book websites that will gladly send your book as a part of a newsletter. Twitter is also amazing. There are so many books out there that dive into the art of promotion, that I'd be doing a disservice if I tried to cover it all here.

Fiverr.com is another way to promote. People will charge 5 dollars to promote your book on the best sites and tweet your book information. Personally I never saw much of a difference in my download numbers, but some people swear by it. Experiment and try everything.

Conclusion

Whether you have an unlimited amount of money to invest or nothing to invest, this business has enough room for everyone who wishes to join. The name of the game is quality and quantity. If you put out good work, people will buy it and you will make good money.

I got started with a couple credit cards and a lot of free time. It turned into an income stream I never imagined. If you don't have money to invest, do as much as you can yourself. It may take a little longer to hit your goal, but you can make it. Every day you wait is a day that your competition is ahead of you.

The game is changing all the time. Stay hungry for information and try new things. If it works, help others with the process. This business isn't about whose throat you can cut. If you write for the right niches, you'll make a ton of money.

Remember that 80% of your money will come from 20% of your books. It's weird but almost always the numbers work out that way. If you release a book that isn't doing well, cut your losses and move on. Don't waste time on books that don't get attention. It's a trial and error kind of game. It doesn't matter if you follow my book to the T, some things you won't truly understand until you've gone through the experience yourself.

It takes patience and perseverance, but honestly if I can make it, anyone can. In the end, it will come down to who wants it more. By reading this book, I already know you do.

Check out these other books by **Phil Johnson** and **D/O PUBLISHING**

http://www.amazon.com/dp/B00U2WP4H0

STAY HUMAN: THE 8 STEPS TO BECOMING A SALES ROCKSTAR by **Phil Johnson**

STAY HUMAN: THE 8 STEPS TO BECOMING A SALES ROCKSTAR is a fantastic guide that will give you the tools you need to get started as a sales person

Are you new to sales? Are you having trouble hitting sales goal or making connections with your customers? You're not alone. There are a lot of sales people out there but for every good salesman there is, there 9 others that aren't. You don't have to be a part of that unskilled pool of talent.

In this book we'll go through 8 steps that will help analyze your interactions, give you tips and exercises to practice so that you'll be a top ranked salesperson in no time!

STAY HUMAN

The book focuses on taking the emphasis off selling a product and focusing on being genuine to build a connection

HOW TO NAVIGATE INTERACTIONS
We go through everything from the first impression to the final goodbye, setting you up for the best success!

DIFFERENT SCENARIOS
We break down different types of interactions and point at what to look for.

If you're just getting started, or need a fresher in the most practical sales techniques, look no further than STAY HUMAN: THE 8 STEPS TO BECOMING A SALES ROCKSTAR

24 STEPS TO GET A PROMOTION: 24 WAYS TO GET THE PROMOTION YOU DESERVE TO MAKE MORE MONEY! By Phil Johnson
http://www.amazon.com/dp/B00VFCW014

24 STEPS TO GET A PROMOTION is a guide to help you move up the ranks at your current job!

It's too easy to get caught doing the same job and growing stagnant. With these 24 steps, you will be on your way to making more money in no time!

In this book we will:

Look at Your Job
We will look at the position you're currently holding and determine if it's a job worth keeping. Then strategize ways to prepare for your rise!

You will learn small steps that will elevate your position, find a mentor, ways to acquire new skills and more!

What are you waiting for!? Grab the book now and start making more money!

GET THE CAREER YOU DESERVE: SET GOALS, FIND A JOB AND GET PAID WHAT YOU'RE WORTH! By **Phil Johnson**

http://www.amazon.com/dp/B00VFDVOWE

GET THE CAREER YOU DESERVE will give you the tools you need to get the career you want!

In this book we will:

SELF ANALYZE
We will take personal inventory and find your strengths and opportunities

SET GOALS
We will determine what goals to set and devise a plan to reach them

RESUME BASICS
We will give you the basic tools to build an effective resume!

BUILD YOUR BRAND
We will analyze ways to build a brand out of your name and give you social proof

FIND A JOB
We will go over ways to find the job you're looking for and how to prepare for it

INTERVIEW
We will go over the tips and tricks as well as 10 Popular interview questions and how to answer them!

and MUCH MORE!

Grab the book now and stop wasting precious time! It's time to get the Career you deserve!

HOW TO THINK LIKE A MILLIONAIRE: TIPS AND TRICKS TO BE MORE PRODUCTIVE AND MAKE BIG MONEY! By **Phil Johnson**

http://www.amazon.com/dp/B00V1QANCW

All we want is to be rich! We want enough money to pay for all of our desires and live a luxurious life with little to no effort. The sad part is that unless you win the lottery, or inherit some money from a wealthy relative, it's not just going to fall into your lap. You have to work for it!

Through out this book, we will explore the thinking of a millionaire and ways that you can adapt so that you can motivate yourself to become more!

We'll reference some of the world's most known millionaires (and some billionaires) while calling you to action to get up and change your life.

What are you waiting for?! Hit the download button now and change your mindset now!

<<<<>>>>

www.ingramcontent.com/pod-product-compliance
Lightning Source LLC
Chambersburg PA
CBHW071018180526

45168CB00003B/1467